Genre Narrative Nonfiction

I0799123

Essential Question

How do we learn about historical events?

BLOWN AWAY

When Krakatoa Exploded

by Andrew Gunn

Introduction

On August 27, 1883, the island of Krakatoa exploded. Smoke and **debris** flew more than 20 miles (32 kilometers) into the sky. The explosion destroyed most of the island. It also created giant **tsunamis** that washed away towns on nearby islands. No one lived on Krakatoa, but thousands of people were killed on the other islands.

Some of the people who saw the eruption did not die. These **survivors** told their stories. This is how we know a lot about what happened when Krakatoa exploded.

THE ILLUSTRATED LONDON NEW

Newspapers around the world reported the eruption of Krakatoa.

The survivors described the terrible damage caused by the explosion. One survivor was a passenger on a ship. Another survivor was a mother caught in a cloud of ash. There was also a worker who ran from a giant wave.

New undersea telegraph cables quickly carried the news of the explosion all over the world. We can learn what the eruption was like when we read news reports and survivors' stories.

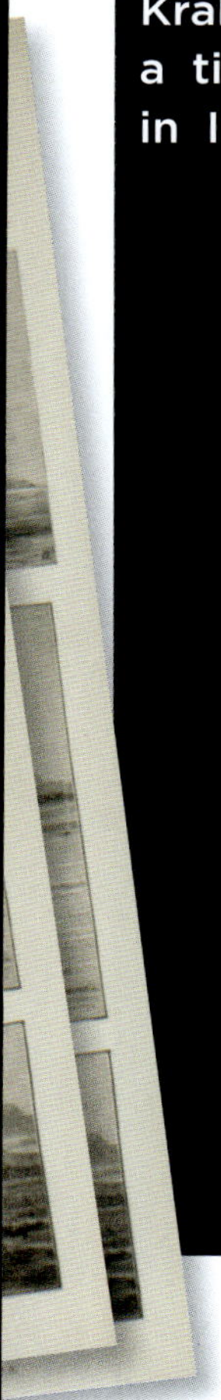

The Location of Krakatoa

Krakatoa is a tiny island in Indonesia.

Chapter 1

Before the Explosion

Sailors could see the island of Krakatoa as they sailed toward Indonesia. The highest point on the island was a volcano called Rakata. It was more than half a mile (813 meters) tall. There were also two smaller **volcanic** cones on the island.

Early in 1883, people living near Krakatoa noticed something strange. They felt **vibrations**, or shaking, from underground. Then, on May 20, a sailor saw a cloud of ash rise high above the island.

Krakatoa Before the Eruption

The island of Krakatoa had three volcanoes. All three were part of the explosion.

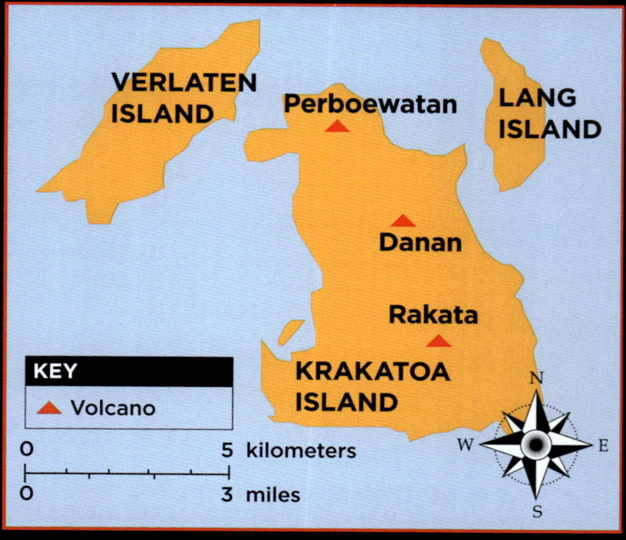

This print shows
Krakatoa before it exploded.

Sailors on other ships also saw strange activity around the island. Ash fell from the sky.

People living nearby became **agitated**. They could see something unusual was happening, and they wanted to know what was going on. Some of them went by boat to Krakatoa to find out. They even climbed up a mountain and looked into a smoking **crater**.

The Pacific Ring of Fire

The Ring of Fire is at the edges of the Pacific Ocean.

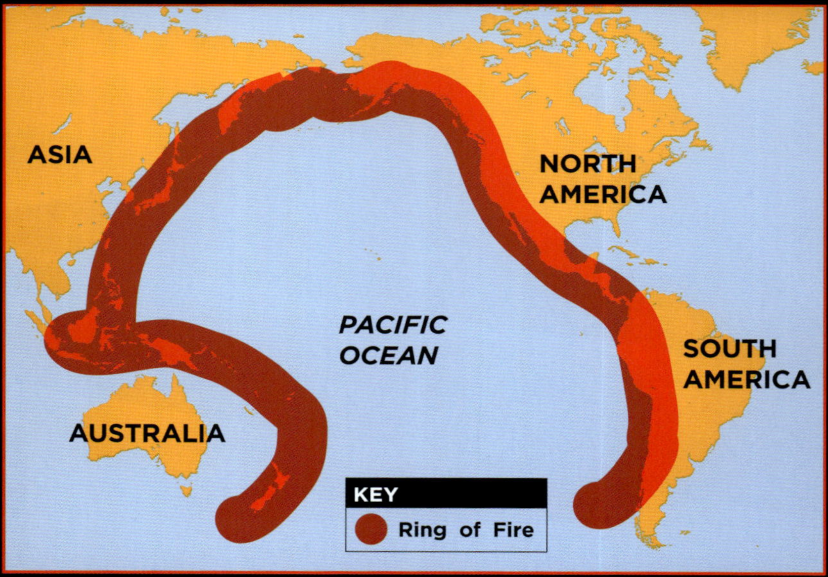

Krakatoa is in an area of the Pacific Ocean called the Ring of Fire. This area has many volcanoes. And there are also many earthquakes.

There are several **tectonic plates** in the Ring of Fire. These plates cause the volcanic and **seismic** activity that happens deep underground.

When two plates push together, one may slip underneath the other. The lower plate **plunges**, or falls, into Earth's mantle. The mantle is the very hot layer beneath Earth's crust. The plate melts and forms hot molten rock called magma.

Pressure builds underground. It pushes the magma up towards Earth's surface. Sometimes magma flows out slowly through openings, or vents, in the crust. Other times, the pressure causes magma to erupt, or explode suddenly out of a vent. Above ground, magma is called **lava**. It cools, hardens, and builds up into a volcano.

The people who looked into the smoking crater on Krakatoa saw the beginning of an eruption. The pressure had not been released yet, so its force was **undiminished**. Soon that force broke out.

A volcano erupts to release pressure.

Know Your Volcanoes

Volcanoes have different shapes.

Stratovolcanoes have steep sides like cones. They are created by eruptions.

Shield volcanoes have wide, flat sides. They form when lava flows slowly in all directions.

Lava domes form when lava piles up at the vent instead of flowing away.

STOP AND CHECK

Why were strange things happening on Krakatoa?

Chapter 2
Krakatoa Explodes

The eruption of Krakatoa was a dramatic sight.

By August 1883, the pressure under Krakatoa was huge. The island began to erupt on Sunday, August 26. The eruption sent smoke 17 miles (27 kilometers) into the air.

Thick clouds of smoke and ash blocked the light from the sun. It grew dark in a town called Anjer. Anjer was 26 miles (42 kilometers) away on the island of Java. The telegraph master in Anjer understood the **urgency** of the situation. He sent a message saying that Krakatoa was "vomiting fire and smoke."

On Monday, August 27, early in the morning, three huge explosions shook the air.

At 10:02 a.m., the whole island of Krakatoa exploded. Some of the island **collapsed**, or fell, into the sea. Rock, magma, gas, and fire blew up into the sky.

The blast may have been the loudest noise ever heard at that time. The captain of a nearby ship wrote down what happened. He said that the blast burst the eardrums of more than half of his crew.

The explosions caused a lot of damage, but the worst was yet to come.

BEFORE ERUPTION

Most of Krakatoa blew into the sky or fell into the sea when it erupted.

AFTER ERUPTION

No one lived on Krakatoa. However, the **populous** islands nearby were badly affected by the explosions.

The volcanoes **ejected** a volcanic rock called pumice. They also threw out hot clouds of gas and ash. The clouds were heavier than air. They traveled across the water at high speed.

These deadly clouds killed about two thousand people. The eruption also caused tsunamis. These giant waves destroyed towns on the islands of Java and Sumatra.

A tsunami carried the steamship Berouw far inland.

For many people, it was **futile** to run from the tsunamis because the waves came so fast. One survivor said, "The wave was too quick ... and many were drowned almost at my side."

Out at sea, the passengers of a ship saw a tsunami destroy the town of Telok Betong. One of them wrote that "... the houses disappeared; the steamer Berouw was lifted and got stuck ... at the height of the cocoanut trees."

The Krakatoa disaster killed more than 36,000 people.

STOP AND CHECK

What happened when Krakatoa erupted?

Chapter 3

Effects Around the World

The effects of Krakatoa's eruption were seen all over the world.

The explosion was heard more than 2,000 miles (3,200 kilometers) away. It changed the air pressure in the atmosphere. It caused a **shock wave** that traveled around the world seven times.

The effects of the eruption were also seen in the sky. **Jet streams** moved ash and dust through the sky.

Light reflected off the ash and dust in the atmosphere. This created beautiful sunsets for months. In England, the painter William Ashcroft made **sketches** and drawings of the sunsets.

People all over the world were **fascinated** and amazed by the size of the eruption on Krakatoa. The news was spread by a new technology called telegraph cables.

William Ashcroft painted this sunset caused by dust from Krakatoa.

Early in the 1800s, before telegraph cables, it took two weeks to get news from across the ocean. However, people around the world read about Krakatoa very quickly. News of the first eruption in May 1883 was reported in *The Times* of London a few days later.

When the island erupted in August, *The New York Times* reported the news within hours. The newspaper said that stones were falling from the sky. The paper added, "It is feared there has been a calamity there."

Telegraph cables were the **crucial** technology that allowed the news to travel so fast. The cables sent messages using Morse code. They sent news almost instantly.

STOP AND CHECK

Why did news of the Krakatoa disaster spread quickly?

Undersea Telegraph Cables

By 1883, undersea telegraph cables connected many far-off places.

Good Timing for Technology

Samuel Morse invented the telegraph in 1836. At the time, cables could be laid only across land. The cables couldn't reach islands such as Java and Sumatra.

In 1850, sap from a tree was used to seal the cables. The sap protected the cables from water and sea life. By the time Krakatoa erupted, there was an undersea cable between Indonesia and Singapore.

Conclusion

The explosion of Krakatoa in 1883 still fascinates people. This is partly because it was one of the worst disasters ever recorded.

There is another reason that people are still interested in Krakatoa. People who were there told about or wrote down their experiences. We can learn what the event was like for them.

After Krakatoa exploded, many people **presumed** that there would be no more eruptions. In 1927, fishermen saw smoke coming from the sea. A new volcanic island had formed. It was named Anak Krakatau, "Child of Krakatoa." It continues to grow, **smoldering** and sometimes erupting.

In 2010, another volcano erupted. This volcano was in Iceland. The people living nearby had to leave the area. Aircraft couldn't fly through the ash, so people all over the world were **stranded**. They were stuck at airports and could not travel.

We learned about this event from newspapers, television, and the Internet. And as with Krakatoa, we learned even more from people's stories.

This volcanic eruption in Iceland caused flights all over the world to be canceled.

Respond to Reading

Summarize

Summarize the effects of the Krakatoa eruption. Use details from *Blown Away*. Your graphic organizer may help you.

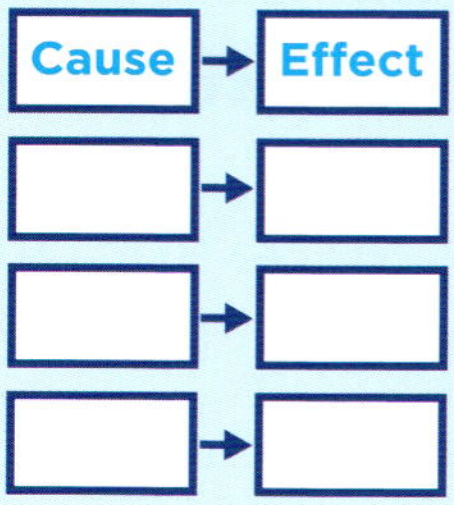

Text Evidence

1. Reread pages 10 and 11. What effects did Krakatoa's explosion have on nearby islands? **CAUSE AND EFFECT**

2. Find the word *mantle* on page 6. What clues help you to figure out the word's meaning? **VOCABULARY**

3. Reread pages 6 and 7. Write about the underground changes that caused Krakatoa to erupt. **WRITE ABOUT READING**

Genre Magazine Article

Compare Texts

Read what one person saw and heard during the Krakatoa eruption.

A Sailor's Story

Captain W. J. Watson was on a ship, the *Charles Bal*, when Krakatoa erupted.

The Atlantic Monthly magazine published an interview with Captain Watson in 1884. These are notes from his record of the events.

At 2:30 P.M., *we noticed some agitation about the point of Krakatoa; clouds or something being propelled [blown] from the north-east ...*

At 4:15 P.M., *... we observed a repetition of [the noise] ... only much more furious and alarming ...*

At 5 the roaring noise continued and was increasing ... darkness spread over the sky, and a hail of pumice-stone fell on us ...

This print shows that people who saw the Krakatoa eruption were in great danger.

At 11 P.M. ... the island, ... eleven miles distant, became visible. Chains of fire appeared to ascend [rise] and descend [fall] between it and the sky, while on the south-west end there seemed to be a continued roll of balls of white fire ...

From midnight to 4 A.M. ... the roaring of Krakatoa less continuous, but more explosive in sound, the sky one second intense blackness and the next a blaze of light ...

At 8:30 ... passed Anjer close enough in to make out the houses, but could see no movement of any kind ... we did not see a single moving thing of any kind on sea or land.

At 11:15 there was a fearful explosion in the direction of Krakatoa, now over thirty miles distant. We saw a wave rush right on to the Button Island, ... sweeping entirely over the southern part, and rising half way up the north and east sides ... and then continuing on to the Java shore ...

At noon the darkness was so intense that we had to grope [feel] our way about the decks ... This horrible state and downpour of mud and debris continued until 1:30 P.M. *...*

... spars, sails, blocks, and ropes were in a horrible state; but ... nobody was hurt nor was the ship damaged. But think of Anjer, Merak, and other little villages on the Java coast!

Make Connections

How does *A Sailor's Story* help you to understand the Krakatoa eruption? **ESSENTIAL QUESTION**

In *Blown Away* and *A Sailor's Story,* how did people around the world learn about the eruption? **TEXT TO TEXT**

Glossary

crater *(KRAY-tuhr)* a bowl-shaped hollow at the top of a volcano ***(page 5)***

debris *(duh-BREE)* the remains of something broken or destroyed ***(page 2)***

jet streams *(jet streems)* high-speed currents of wind that travel between layers of the atmosphere ***(page 13)***

lava *(LAH-vuh)* magma ejected from a volcano ***(page 7)***

seismic *(SIGHZ-mik)* caused by an earthquake or explosion ***(page 6)***

shock wave *(shahk wayv)* a wave of high-pressure air caused by an explosion or earthquake ***(page 12)***

tectonic plates *(tek-TAH-nik playts)* pieces of Earth's outer crust; they cover Earth's surface like giant jigsaw pieces ***(page 6)***

tsunamis *(tsoo-NAH-meez)* huge waves caused by an eruption or earthquake under the ocean ***(page 2)***

volcanic *(vahl-KAN-ik)* formed or produced by a volcano ***(page 4)***

Index

Focus on
Social Studies

Purpose To understand how primary sources can help us picture a historical event

What to do

Step 1 Work in pairs. Choose a historical event that interests you, such as the moon landing or Hurricane Katrina.

Step 2 Write down everything you know about the event. Include dates, people, and actions.

Step 3 Find two primary sources of information about the event. A primary source is something that was created at the time of the event, not later. It could be a newspaper report, a map, or a photograph.

Step 4 What new information did you get from your primary sources? Were some of the things you wrote down when you started incorrect?

Conclusion How do primary sources make a historical event more interesting?